classic·festival·solos

MW00576481

Contents

CLASSIC FESTIVAL SOLOS, Volume 2 is a counterpart to the companion, Volume 1. Idiomatic solo materials with an eye to variety and playability are included, beginning with easier material and progressing to more difficult.

Works from several periods of composition are presented to give the advancing student the opportunity to learn and to demonstrate performance in each appropriate style. Technical progression is taken into consideration as well as program appeal for both soloist and audience.

Jack Lamb, Editor

To Guido Fucinari

VALSE "AU PRINTEMPS"

LEONARD B. SMITH, ASCAP

Copyright © 1973 BELWIN MILLS PUBLISHING CORP., c/o CPP/BELWIN, INC., Miami, FL 33014

4

DEDICATION

WILLIAM PELZ

5

6

EL03888

ANDANTINO

FERNANDO SOR
Transcribed by R. CHRISTIAN DISHINGER

* *Staccato markings should be interpreted as separation between notes rather than extreme short notes.*

8

EL03888

9

EL03888

CHORALE MELODY No. 19*

J.S. BACH
Arranged by LEONARD B. SMITH

This is from the "69 CHORALE MELODIES" with figured bass, originally published in 1832 as an addendum to the 371 Chorales. It is known as "MEIN JESU! was für Seelenweh" (My Jesus, how great anguish of soul).

It is a beautiful piece and should be played with great attention to the markings.

SCARLATTI SUITE
I
Allegro

A. SCARLATTI (1660-1725)
Arranged by BERNARD FITZGERALD

14

II
Adagio

III
Allegro

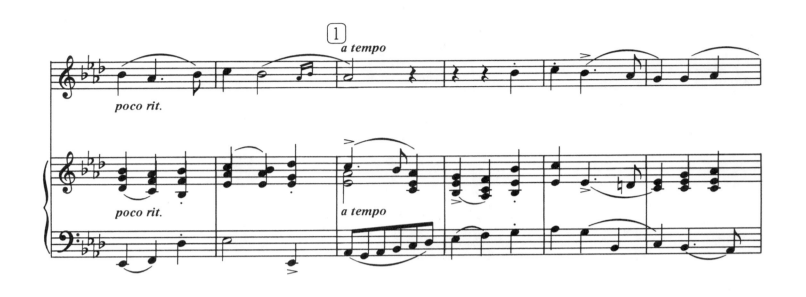

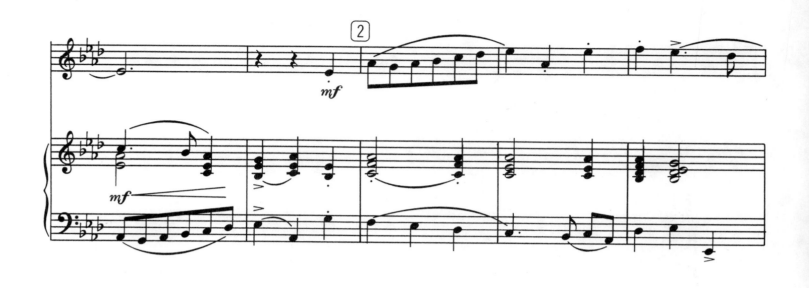

ARIA
Bist du bei mir
If Thou be Near

J.S. BACH
Arranged by BERNARD FITZGERALD

LA CASA

GERALD KNIPFEL - BELDON LEONARD

Copyright © 1958 (Renewed 1986) BELWIN MILLS PUBLISHING CORP., c/o CPP/BELWIN, INC., Miami, FL 33014
International Copyright Secured   Made in U.S.A.   All Rights Reserved

Andante con expressione

E Allegretto con moto

EL VERANO

GERALD KNIPFEL - BELDON LEONARD

EL03888

Andante espressivo

Allegro con brio

Dedicated to my wife

INTRODUCTION AND FANTASY

BERNARD FITZGERALD

Copyright © 1940 (Renewed 1968) BELWIN MILLS PUBLISHING CORP., c/o CPP/BELWIN, INC., Miami, FL 33014
International Copyright Secured   Made in U.S.A.   All Rights Reserved

For Ernest A. Jones

HAPPY GO LUCKY

LEONARD B. SMITH, ASCAP

To Robert K. Collins

ROAD RUNNER

LEONARD B. SMITH, ASCAP

45

EL03888

THE EASY WINNERS

SCOTT JOPLIN
Edited by BOBBY HERRIOT
Arranged by HOWARD CABLE

Easy rag-time tempo (not fast)

Volume I

CLASSIC FESTIVAL SOLOS, Volume I offers the advancing instrumental soloist an array of materials, graded from easy to more challenging. An assortment of musical styles has been included to give variety and to allow an opportunity for the musician to develop interpretive skills. Many of the solos included appear on State Contest lists.

CLASSIC FESTIVAL SOLOS are available for 16 instruments, each with piano accompaniment. In addition, a book of unaccompanied snare drum solos is offered as part of this series.

Instrumentation:

C FLUTE
____ (EL03720) **Solo Book**
____ (EL03721) **Piano Accompaniment**

OBOE
____ (EL03722) **Solo Book**
____ (EL03723) **Piano Accompaniment**

B♭ CLARINET
____ (EL03724) **Solo Book**
____ (EL03725) **Piano Accompaniment**

E♭ ALTO CLARINET
____ (EL03726) **Solo Book**
____ (EL03727) **Piano Accompaniment**

B♭ BASS CLARINET
____ (EL03728) **Solo Book**
____ (EL03729) **Piano Accompaniment**

BASSOON
____ (EL03730) **Solo Book**
____ (EL03731) **Piano Accompaniment**

E♭ ALTO SAXOPHONE
____ (EL03732) **Solo Book**
____ (EL03733) **Piano Accompaniment**

B♭ TENOR SAXOPHONE
____ (EL03734) **Solo Book**
____ (EL03735) **Piano Accompaniment**

E♭ BARITONE SAXOPHONE
____ (EL03736) **Solo Book**
____ (EL03737) **Piano Accompaniment**

B♭ TRUMPET
____ (EL03738) **Solo Book**
____ (EL03739) **Piano Accompaniment**

HORN IN F
____ (EL03740) **Solo Book**
____ (EL03741) **Piano Accompaniment**

TROMBONE
____ (EL03742) **Solo Book**
____ (EL03743) **Piano Accompaniment**

BARITONE (Bass Clef)
____ (EL03744) **Solo Book**
____ (EL03745) **Piano Accompaniment**

TUBA
____ (EL03746) **Solo Book**
____ (EL03747) **Piano Accompaniment**

MALLET PERCUSSION
____ (EL03748) **Solo Book**
____ (EL03749) **Piano Accompaniment**

SNARE DRUM
____ (EL03750) **Solo Book**
____ (EL03751) **Piano Accompaniment**

SNARE DRUM
____ (EL03752) **Solo Book (Unaccompanied)**